THE

PEOPLE'S PRIMER

OF

CHURCH PRINCIPLES.

NEW EDITION, ENLARGED,

WITH NOTES ON CHRISTIAN ANTIQUITIES AND
MODERN RITUALISM.

COMPILED BY THE

REV. A. KING.

London:
ELLIOT STOCK, 62, PATERNOSTER ROW, E.C.

UNWIN BROTHERS, PRINTERS, CHILWORTH AND LONDON.

INTRODUCTORY NOTES.

The following pages have not been written in the interests of sectarian controversy.

They are designed, rather, to prevent bitter disputation, and to promote godly edifying, peace, and concord, by a calm appeal to the Word of God.

Yet it is evident that the inquiry here instituted, has an important bearing both on the conflicts of the sects and on the great national question concerning the relations of any sect, or of any section of the clergy, to the Government of the State.

"CHURCH PRINCIPLES" are commanding the attention of earnest minds in every part of Christendom, and the discussion of them is likely to become, more than ever, the controversy of the age.

Happily, the subject is now regarded as more important and more sacred, than mere sectaries, or political partisans, would make it.

It is not a frivolous criticisim of sectarian definitions, ritual symbols, religious forms, or modes of worship.

It is more than a question of police. Its highest use and application are not to be found in quelling a clerical mutiny, or enforcing subordination on a refractory wing of the Civil Service.

CHURCH PRINCIPLES involve a grave inquiry regarding the Divine origin and authority of Christianity.

Is the Gospel of our Salvation revealed in Holy Scripture in connection with distinctive principles of Christian fellowship, for the formation and guidance of Christian Churches? or, is the Christian religion to be regarded as largely consisting of merely human inventions, the impositions of statesmanship or priest-craft, or the expedients of devout ambition, evolved from the superstition or philosophy of successive generations, for the exaltation of the clergy and the subjection of mankind?

Most serious persons will admit that if the Christian revelation provides for its own propagation in the world, it is important to ascertain its Ordinances; and obviously wise and right to adopt the Divine rule, rather than invent and impose another.

"TO THE LAW, AND TO THE TESTIMONY."—What saith the Scripture?

Can the authority of the New Testament be fairly pleaded in support of the clerical hierarchies and elaborate systems of ecclesiastical uniformity and histrionic ritual, which have prevailed in Christendom?

Every candid student of the Bible, will admit that none of these things were enjoined by Christ and His Apostles.

Every candid student of Ecclesiastical History knows that they are usurpations and impositions of human authority; that they originated in an erroneous imitation of the Levitical ceremonial, which the New Testament condemns; and in an adroit appropriation of the spoils of Imperial Paganism, by a corrupt and ambitious priesthood.

Some devout and thoughtful persons have earnestly inquired whether "organized Christianity" is of God.

The sad history of spiritual despotism, materialistic formalism, and gross superstition, which have assumed the name of Christianity, lends a terrible significance to this inquiry; and, certainly, if we had no alternative between these and the uncovenanted, unaffiliated isolation of individual "believers," we must meet the inquiry by a solemn and emphatic—"No."

The corrupt organizations of the post-Apostolic and Middle Ages, which have survived and developed themselves even in our own times, and now oppose themselves alike to Scriptural Christianity and human progress, are *not* of God.

Although He has permitted them, and in His Sovereign mercy condescends to bless and work with the truth and conscience that are in them, yet they must perish, in order that the Gospel of Christ may prevail and His kingdom be established in the world.

"But "fellowship in the Gospel" is as distinctly set forth in Holy Scripture, as is the Gospel itself. (Phil. i. 5.)

While the New Testament prescribes no ritual or forms of worship, it clearly enjoins and records association amongst Christian worshippers.

Apostolic Christianity treated not only of Christ, but of "Christ and the Church." Nay, the very nature and design of the Gospel are presented by the inspired Apostles of our Lord and Saviour, in connection with the institution and action, the life and work, the privileges and duties, the faults, the failures, and the fortunes of those whom God had "called unto the fellowship of his Son Jesus Christ our Lord" (1 Cor. i. 9), and who, by Divine charter and ordinance, are "no more strangers and foreigners, but fellow citizens with the Saints, and of the household of God, . . . builded together for an habitation of God, through the Spirit." (Ephes. ii. 19-22.)

We cannot adequately learn what is New Testament Christianity, unless we become acquainted with New Testament Churches.

It is perfectly certain that our Lord and His Apostles did not ordain any system or canons of ecclesiastical uniformity, or set up any Church as a model, in all matters of order and detail, for the promotion of organized Christianity.*

* "No such thing is to be found in our Scriptures as a Catechism, or regular elementary Introduction to the Christian religion ; nor do they furnish us with anything of the nature of a systematic creed, set of articles, or confession of faith.

"Neither, again, do they supply us with a Liturgy for ordinary Public Worship, or with forms of administering the Sacraments, or of conferring Holy Orders ; nor do they even give us any precise directions as to these and other ecclesiastical matters, or anything that at all corresponds to a rubric or set of canons. . . .

"Since no one of the first promulgators of Christianity did what they must have been *naturally* led to do, it follows that they must have been *supernaturally* withheld from doing it.

"That a number of Jews, accustomed from infancy to a strict Ritual, should, in introducing Christianity, as the second part of the same Dispensation, have abstained, not only from accurately prescribing for the use of all Christian Churches for ever, the mode of Divine Worship, but even from recording what was actually in use under their own directions, does seem to me utterly incredible, unless we suppose them to have been restrained from doing this, by a special admonition of the Divine spirit. . . .

"Supposing such a summary to have been drawn up, it would have generated a careless and contented apathy. There would have been no call for a vigilant investigation of the truth. In fact all study, properly so called, of the rest of Scripture, all lively interest in its perusal, would have been entirely superseded.

"Orthodoxy would have been petrified, cold, unchangeable, lifeless.

"While the *principles* which Christian communities are to act upon, are clearly recognized and strongly inculcated, *the precise mode* in which they are to be acted upon, are left undefined.

"To the Church, then, has her All-Wise Founder left the office of teaching ; to the Scriptures that of proving, the Christian doctrines : to the Scriptures He has left the delineation of Christian *principles* : TO EACH CHURCH the application of those principles."

———————

* *Archbishop Whately's* " Peculiarities of the Christian Religion" —" *Essay on Omissions*,"—pp. 203, 214, 221.

But it is also perfectly certain that they did enact certain elementary principles and fundamental rules, as the common law of Christian fellowship, for the formation and government of every Christian Church.

All Churches are free, by Divine ordinance, to adopt any order that is in harmony with these first principles.

No Church is free to set these Divine institutions aside, or to overlay and neutralize them, by any observances, of the traditions and commandments of men.

Any Church, systematically violating or ignoring them, is guilty of rebellion against Christ, who is the head ; and commits the sin of schism against His body, which is the Church. (Rom. xii. ; 1 Cor. xii. ; Ephes. iv. v. ; 1 Peter ii.)

The simplicity of New Testament Church principles has led some to overlook their true significance, and to question the Divine ordinance of "organized Christianity."

But it is in this simplicity their Divine origin appears, as constituting a "perfect law of liberty," teaching Christians to be "subject one to another," and yet to "call no man master;" and binding all believers of the same glorious Gospel, to an allegiance of holy brotherhood, by one Divine canon,—

"ONE IS YOUR MASTER, EVEN CHRIST; AND ALL YE ARE BRETHREN"! (Matt. xxiii. 8.)

In the adoption and prevalence of these principles, must be formed a true "Catholic Church," in "the communion of Saints," of every nation of mankind.

By the acceptance of these principles only, and not by the imposition of any ritual uniformity, is it possible for Christianity ever to become truly catholic.

The leaves of every tree, in every forest, in every part of the world, may as soon be cut and clipped, and kept to one pattern, as the living men of all nations can be,—intellectually, morally, educationally, and in all their religious manhood,—stretched, or stunted, or squeezed into one formula of faith and worship.

But wherever the word of the truth of the Gospel is received by men in the love of it, and is made the power of God unto salvation, it brings forth fruit in them, after its kind.

Spiritual fruits, amongst people of different nations and from age to age, will be,—as are the natural fruits of various climates,—of great diversity; and the methods of their culture, as well as the times and modes of their ingathering and their use, will be alike various; so that the right or the best mode for one place or time, may prove to be wrong, or even the worst, for another.

But as they are all of "God's husbandry," they will all be good fruit—"fruits of righteousness by Jesus Christ, unto the glory and praise of God" (Phil. i. 11).

A Christian negro may, in many things, differ from a Christian Hindoo, as an Englishman differs from either and from both; or as a Chinaman or a Turk differs from a Frenchman or a North American Indian.

But the essentials of true Christianity, as the elements of a new life, will be the same in all.

As the Gospel of the grace of God "turns them from darkness to light, and from the power of Satan unto God," they are all the children of God by faith in Christ Jesus. And as the instinct of the new birth in each, is to cry unto God, "Abba, Father," so, in their several spheres and circumstances of spiritual growth to Christian manhood, realising that there is *one celestial tongue amongst the many languages of mortals* ("Πολλαι μεν θνητοις γλωτται, μια δ' Αθανατοισιν"), they can all, in various forms of utterance, and amidst various conditions of social life, intelligently adopt the language of the great Apostle of the nations:—" I bow my knees unto the

Father of our Lord Jesus Christ, of whom the whole family in heaven and earth is named."

The simple "Church principles" of the New Testament, meet and satisfy the social wants of the Christian life. They commend themselves to Christian common sense, and the yearning of every Christian heart, for fellowship with kindred spirits, in work and worship.

They help fellow-disciples to walk together in love, " endeavouring to keep the unity of the spirit in the bond of peace ;" and they provide the only effectual means of forming a true Catholic Church, because they can be adopted in all conditions of human life, in connection with every state of society, every degree of culture and civilization, and every form of government, among all the nations of mankind, until the kingdoms of this world shall become the kingdoms of our Lord and of His Christ, and the whole earth shall be filled with His glory.

As the greatest system of error and Apostacy in Christendom, has effectually commended its impositions and shielded its enormities, by pleading the authority of the Church, and as I have had the honour to conduct the last discussion (likely to remain as *the last*), with a fully equipped and regularly appointed champion of the Papacy, on this subject, it is proper for me to record how a clear and logical treatment of the question, baffles the tactics of priestcraft, and secures for Scriptural Christianity, an easy victory over all the forces of Rome.

One of the most eminent of the Anglican leaders of the new Apostacy to Popery, an Oxford scholar, a clergyman of our National Establishment, brother of an English Earl, the Hon. and Rev. G. Spencer, went with Drs. Newman and Manning, from the training-school of Dr. Pusey, to become a liegeman of the Pope.

Having been re-ordained and subjected to four years' special training in Rome, this gentleman returned, on a special mission for the conversion of British Protestants to the Church of Rome; and armed with the Pope's patent and an indulgence for all who might aid and pray for the success of his labours, he visited the city in which I then resided, and proceeded to his task, by inviting his clerical brethren of the Established Church, to follow his example, and find peace and unity in the Roman Catholic Communion.

As I had been previously seeking, in vain, to induce Roman Catholic clergymen to assist me in discussing the true Catholic faith, and unfolding the true idea of the Christian Church, to the people, and as multitudes were moved with earnest inquiries on the subject, I immediately waited on our illustrious visitor, showed him the state of the case, and urged him to the discharge of his chosen duty, as champion of the Papacy.

After several weeks' private intercourse and reiterated public invitations to discussion, on my part, which he met by persistent but hesitating refusals, at length my friend received permission from Rome; and, having amicably arranged preliminaries, returned to London, avowedly for the purpose of having Cardinal Wiseman's assistance, in his discussion with me, which he had stipulated to be weekly, through the newspaper press.

After a few weeks' work, my learned opponent began to waver; and soon after, under the advice of his astute superior, he found an excuse for proceeding to the Continent, and precipitately fled from the conflict, leaving me master of the field.

Our subject of discussion was "The Church." I arraigned the Papacy as a usurpation, and demanded definitions and proofs of the authority and infallibility, claimed for the Church of Rome.

My friend had been received and appointed by the Pope,

before the Vatican decree had made the Pope infallible. He did not hold the Pope's infallibility, although he was the Pope's appointed champion and representative. But I had previously maintained that Romanism must come to that, and that the Infallibility of the Pope was the logical issue and only possible completion of its impracticable and contradictory assumptions.

Of course I pressed my opponent to this issue. He had taken his ground on the old theory, of *the Infallibility of the Church*. In reply to my interrogatories, " What is the Catholic Church ? and how does the Church of Rome establish her own claim to Supremacy, Unity, and Infallibility?" he defined the Catholic Church as " a body of people of all nations, who believe a certain form of doctrines," &c., and distinctly fenced his own position by stating, " It is not the Church of Rome, strictly speaking, which I defend ; but the Catholic Church spread throughout the world;" . . . and, again, " I assert Supremacy to be the attribute of the Church, or rather of the Bishop, of Rome ; Unity and Infallibility of the Catholic Church." *

Here, then, was *the last battle of the old Papacy*. My retort was inevitable. If the Catholic Church be a body of people, and if Infallibility is the attribute of the Catholic Church, then a body of people is infallible. If the Bishop of Rome, who is not infallible, be supreme ruler of the Infallible Church, then is not truth enslaved by power ? and how can the decisions of the Infallible Church be infallibly expressed through the errors and corruptions of the Papacy ?

Moreover, even if there were an infallible authority in the Church on earth, what would it avail for the masses of mankind ?

The oracle, however sacred, might still be misunderstood.

* " Protestantism and the Church of Rome." Discussion between the Hon. and Rev. G. Spencer and the Rev. A. King. Pp. 15, 17, 22, 30, 33.

Our blessed Lord was misunderstood, often even by His own disciples. Holy Scripture is liable to be misunderstood. We are perpetually assured that the Church and the Pope are misunderstood.

What does the alleged Infallibility accomplish? and where does it reside? If the supreme authority is Infallible, we must admit the Pope's Infallibility. If the Church is Infallible, we must recognise the authority of the people, because the people constitute the Church.

My learned friend, having become involved in the toils of this plain argument, could extricate himself only by flight.

He fled, and reported his discomfiture in Rome, and thus contributed to hasten the issuing of the Vatican decree, making the Infallibility of the Pope an article of the Romish faith, which doctrine he had, in the name and by the authority of the Pope, emphatically repudiated and denied!

While sincerely deploring the lamentable results of a departure from the simplicity of the Gospel, manifested in the career of my learned and respected antagonist, and gratefully cherishing the hope that, in his bitter disappointment and humiliation, he ultimately found rest for his soul in Christ, I feel bound to urge the great lesson, afforded by his case, upon all who are set for the defence of Scriptural Christianity.

Not by bitter sectarian strife, not by intolerant and abusive charges of "idolatry" and "blasphemy" (even when these awful terms appear to be warranted), but by calm, charitable, courteous, yet cogent and inexorable, argument, *on the basis of admitted truth*, can devout and earnest souls be won from the delusions of superstition, to the light and liberty of the Gospel of Christ.

It is a great joy to be able to record the complete overthrow of Rome's master fallacy of "Church authority," by a fair discussion with a Goliath of the Papacy, on the simple question of "The Church."

This is the great question of the age. It is shaking to pieces the old kingdoms of the old Roman Empire, and giving warning to "things that are shaken," of the coming of "a kingdom which cannot be moved."

The new order of human affairs, that will succeed the next great overthrow of European state-craft and priestly imposture, will assuredly vindicate the supremacy of Christ and the liberty of His Church :—and then, the grandest confederations of human power will appear to be but bungling impostures, as compared with the Divine simplicity and efficiency of "fellowship in the Gospel."

There is now no middle ground, logically tenable, between the newest edition of the Papacy, and the old Christianity, taught by Christ and His Apostles.

The real issue in Christendom to-day—on which all men have to make a choice—is between the impossibilities of the Pope's official Infallibility, and the "Church principles" of the New Testament.

The only Infallibility of the Church on earth, is that which all honest, earnest, humble-minded Christians may attain, by the teaching of God's Spirit, through the study of God's word, in the obedience of faith, and by the interpretation and application of Christian candour and common sense.

By these all-sufficient means of Divine conservatism, the Lord Christ fulfils His promise to His Church, that "the gates of hell shall not prevail against it."

The sad defection from Evangelical truth, which has prevailed so extensively in our National Established Church, very painfully illustrates the importance of a faithful adherence to New Testament Church principles.

Remarks of eminent men, whose impartiality will be admitted, are introduced here, not in a spirit of hostility, but for salutary warning and instruction.

Archbishop Whately, with a candour equal to his logical discrimination, judiciously, and almost *judicially* declares :

"Those whose 'Church principles' lead them to remove from a firm foundation, the institutions of a Christian Church, and especially of our own, and to place them on the sand, are moreover compelled, as it were, with their own hands, to dig away even that very foundation of sand. . . . Instead of a clearly intelligible, well-established, and accessible proof f Divine sanction for the claims of our Church, they would substitute one that is not only obscure, disputable, and out of the reach of the mass of mankind, but even self-contradictory, subversive of our own and every Church's claims, and leading to the very evils of doubt and schismatical division, which it is desired to guard against. . . .

"It is advancing, but not in the right road; it is advancing, not in sound learning, but in error—not in faith, but in superstitious credulity, to seek for some higher and better ground on which to rest our doctrines and institutions, than that on which they were placed by 'the Author and Finisher of our faith.'"

Again, the Archbishop pointedly remarks: "It is curious to observe how very common it is for a sect or party to assume a title indicative of the very excellence in which they are especially deficient, or strongly condemnatory of the very errors with which they are especially chargeable. . . .

"The phrase 'Catholic religion' (*i.e.*, universal) is most commonly in the mouths of those who are most limited and *exclusive* in their views, and who seek to shut out the largest number of Christian communities, from the Gospel covenant. 'Schism,' again, is by none more loudly reprobated than by those who are not only the immediate authors of schism, but the advocates of principles tending to generate and perpetuate schisms without end. And 'Church principles,' 'High Church principles,' 'Church of England principles,' are the favourite terms of those who go the furthest in subverting all these. Obvious as this fallacy is, there is none more commonly successful in throwing men off their guard. . . .

" One may not unfrequently hear members of Episcopalian Churches pronouncing severe condemnation on those of other communions, and even excluding them from the Christian body, on the ground of their wanting the very essentials of a Christian Church, viz., the very same orders in the hierarchy which (as they allege) the Apostles appointed ; and this while the Episcopalians themselves have, universally, so far varied from the Apostolic institution, as to have, in one Church, several bishops, each of whom, consequently, differs in the office he holds, in a most important point, from one of the primitive bishops. . . .

" The edifice they overthrow, crushes, in its fall, the blind champion who has broken its pillars." *

The learned author of " Ancient Christianity and the Oxford Tracts," has rendered immense service to Christianity, by tracing the Anglican apostacy to its true origin and historical parentage.

" Misunderstanding has arisen, in a material point, from the unavoidable vagueness of the phrase ' Ancient Christianity.' . . .

" It is manifest that while the English Reformers rejected with religious indignation, the corruptions of the fourth century, *which they strangely regarded as of later origin*, they thought themselves quite secure from the infection of the great apostacy, when they had travelled back on the track of ages, so far as the suffering age of the Church, which they fondly believed to be ' pure and holy.' . . .

" The worship, the sacramental notions, and the feeling, of the African Church, of the time of Cyprian, furnished the ideal model, which the founders of the English Church held in their view.   With these notions and practices, which affect the

---

* *Archbishop Whately's* "Kingdom of Christ," p. 113, 114, 127, 130, 131.

offices,' were mingled the very incongruous materials proper to
the Continental reformation. I mean those energetic Evangelic
principles which gave life to the preaching of Luther and his
colleagues. Almost an utter dissimilarity distinguishes the
Christianity of Luther from that of Cyprian, and yet elements
of both are bound together in the same prayer-book and
homilies.

"From this source have arisen, from time to time, *differences
which no ingenuity of explanation can ever avail to reconcile;*
and feuds to which, in the nature of things, no method of
pacification can be applied. . . .

" It is thus at this moment. Cyprian and Luther are
wrestling amain, for mastery in the English Church; and the
one or the other of these spirits *must be dislodged.*

" A season of apathy may again come upon the Church, and
so the struggle may stand over to another day; but at its
next revival, the English Church will either go over uncon-
ditionally to 'antiquity,' erasing from its formularies whatever
is Protestant, and will expel all who adhere to Scriptural
doctrine, or it will recover its lost ground, and become con-
sistently Protestant and Biblical. . . .

" The Oxford writers—inconsiderately and, as we may believe, in ignorance—committed themselves to the task of
restoring the doctrines and usages of the fourth century. But
asceticism was a main element of this scheme ; this, therefore,
must be promoted and defended, whether it be good or bad;
and how bad it actually was, they did not clearly discover, until
too late.

"That very period which is the most perplexing, the period
during which the true glory of the Christian system was
bartered for worldly power, and its purity betrayed, and its
honour compromised—this period has been selected, by the ill-
judging writers with whom we have to do, and held up as the
object of unconditional veneration and imitation. . . . .

"A system of effective falsification has been resorted to for the purpose of carrying forward the scheme which is intended to supplant the Reformation and to restore to the English Church, the superstitions which it had rejected. . . . Before we reprobate Popes, Councils, and Romanist Saints, let us fairly see what sort of system it was, which the Doctors and Martyrs of the highest antiquity, had delivered into their care and custody. We Protestants are prompt enough to condemn the Pontiffs or St. Bernard; but let inquiry be made concerning the Christianity embodied in the writings of those to whom Popes and Doctors looked up, as their undoubted masters. The Church of Rome has done the best it could, to bring the cumbrous abomination, bequeathed to it by the Saints and Doctors and Martyrs of the pristine age, into a manageable condition.

"When the condition of the Christianised, and yet Pagan, mass of the fourth and fifth centuries—so far as it can at this time be understood—is compared with that of Roman Catholic communities in the sixteenth and seventeenth centuries, I am prepared to affirm that modern Romanism is a reform upon ancient Christianity—that is the Christianity of the closing years of the fourth century. . . .

"Carefully considering the Christianity of that very period which has been held up by the Oxford writers, as a fit object of devout imitation, I deliberately affirm that it were far better for a community, to submit itself to modern Romanism—in doctrine, Government, and discipline—than to pass into the ecclesiastical condition, which belonged to the Eastern, the Western, and the African Churches, in the fourth and fifth centuries. . . .

"Those who at this time are endeavouring to revive the obsolete Saint-worship, plead, 'We wish only to carry out the Church system.'

"'The Church,' thought of in this instance, by the restorers of 'antiquity,' is very far from being the Protestant Church by law established. It is the so-called 'Catholic Church,' the Church of the fourth, fifth, sixth, and seventh centuries.

Thus regarded, and thus standing forth in shadowy radiance before those of the clergy who are carrying forward ' Church principles,' the dead names of the Calendar, brighten into life : these Saints and Martyrs are all bestirring themselves, and snuffing the wind, for that incense, of which they have been, in these islands, so long defrauded. . . .

" The Calendar, coupled with the ambiguous sense reserved for the term ' the Church,' and with the professed approval of invocation and relic devotion, is, to the Church of England, the INTROIT of a Polytheistic worship." *

Here, then, is the true answer to the inquiry, " What and whence is the Anglican Ritualistic Apostacy?" . . . It is the natural offspring of the Romanism and Patristic pietism, preserved in the Church of England. Its sources and its sanction are to be found in the canons, constitution, and ritual, of our Protestant establishment.

The figments of " priest's orders," baptismal regeneration, and Apostolical succession, give character to the system ; and while elements of Protestantism are mixed up with these, as Christianity is mixed with Paganism in the Church of Rome, its clerical " orders " distinctly testify its relations to Papal hierarchy.

It might seem incredible that a reformed Church should fraternize with Rome, against the reformed Churches ; but the Church of England does more than this : it accepts Romish " ordination ;" while Rome, with a proud consistency of arrogant intolerance, rejects its claims to " clergy," " sacrament," and " Church." It acknowledges Rome as the fountain of clerical " orders," while Rome repudiates its " orders ; " and it then unites with Rome, in ignoring the " orders," and denying the validity of the ministry, of the Protestant Churches of Christendom.

* " Ancient Christianity and the Doctrines of the Oxford Tracts." By Isaac Taylor. Pp. 80, 81, 108, 110. Supplement, pp. 69, 70.

"Without all contradiction, the less is blessed of the better." Our "Church of England" constitutionally proclaims the superiority of the "Church of Rome;" and bids Protestantism croach before the Papacy, with a halter on its head!

In view of this sad state of things, Mr. Taylor—already quoted—suggests some remedial measures, which might be practically important, if the Episcopal "Church" were free to reform herself, or amend her own system.

"From the formularies of the Church, what is glaringly false in fact, should be expunged; and what is at once true in itself, and *necessary to the argumentative existence and consistency of the Church*, should be insisted on and retained. But how momentous would be the consequences of so reasonable an expurgation!

"Were the formularies of the Church relieved of blemishes, which in fact ought to be removed, in regard merely to the literary reputation of so erudite a communion, then would its adversaries on either hand, lose their advantage in argument; and, more than this, the Church would cease to generate, as it has done, and does at this moment, an intestinal plague, threatening its very life."

"The LAITY of the Episcopal Church should be taken by the hand and *restored* to their place, and to their just influence, as the living, conscious, voluntary constituents, of that 'congregation of faithful men,' to which the Church itself has applied the definition of 'A CHURCH.'

"A renovation of our Episcopal Church, such as this, might have an effect upon the deliberations of Rome, similar to that which resulted from the arming and training of the people when England was threatened with invasion.—The *enemy was appalled*, and DESISTED FROM HIS PROJECT.*

These faithful and friendly criticisms, from the most emi-

* "Ancient Christianity," p. 382, and Supplement, p. 48

nently qualified advisers, deserve the immediate and practical acceptance of all honest Protestant and patriotic members of the National Church of England.

The fatal error of our English Reformers, arose from their not knowing the true character of that corrupt "Catholic antiquity," which preceded and produced the Papacy.

By taking the ante-Romish "development" of an intolerant and Paganized era, as their model, they became unconsciously bound to all the logical issues of the theory to which they had subscribed, *and of the Papal claims, which they had rejected!* Thus they virtually surrendered to their adversaries, in what should have been the crisis of their victory ; and thus, *they prepared the way, for the Anglican defection, of the present time.*

A true reformation, must reject, not only the blasphemous assumptions of the Vatican, and the impossibilities of the new religious of Rome, but also the authority and teaching of the filthy dreamers,—the fanatical formalists,—the impure ascetics, —the intolerant persecutors,—the Polytheistic relic-worshippers, and cursing creed-makers, of the Nicene Church.

Whoever would maintain pure Christianity and *Christian* "Church principles," must have the conscience and the courage, to go back from Nicea to Nazareth ; and to *renounce Constantine,*—for CHRIST !

ADVERTISEMENT TO THE BRIGHTON EDITION.

——◆◇◆——

This "Outline of New Testament Church Principles" was at first designed only for the use of my own congregation; being a revised reprint of a little tract which I used, with good effect, several years ago, in my first pastorate.

Not knowing of any other manual, which puts the same subject, with sufficient simplicity and comprehensiveness, before Church Members and inquirers, for the defence and confirmation of the Truth, I am induced, at the suggestion of friends, to offer this, for more general use and more extensive usefulness.

This is not an effort of controversial criticism. My object is a very simple and practical one. Conscientiously believing that Congregational Independency is *not a sectarian system*,—but essentially, and *jure Divino*, the proper "order" of Church fellowship, and, as such, opposed to all sectarianism,—I desire to distinguish it from sectarian error, and to commend it as DIVINE CATHOLIC TRUTH; most fitted to promote Christian liberty and Christian union, Christian orthodoxy and Christian activity, the edification of the Churches and the Evangelisation of the world.

The inquiry here answered is, NOT, "What does *our Church* teach?" or, "What are the peculiar views or usages of *our Denomination?*" but, "What is inculcated upon *all Christians*, in THE WORD OF GOD ?"

I affectionately commend this distinction to all who pray "for the good estate of the Catholic Church ; " to all who hope for the answer of the Redeemer's prayer, that "all" His people "may be one" in faith and love; one in Him, and one in scriptural effort, for the promotion of His glory and the establishment of HIS KINGDOM.

A. K.

——————

. *The texts of Scripture should be taken, not as separate proofs, but as connected illustrations of the statements to which they are severally attached.*

OUTLINE OF

New Testament Church Principles.

— ◆ —

A CHRISTIAN CHURCH

Is a voluntary Society of professed Christians, uniting together for the Worship of God, the observance of Christian Ordinances, and the promotion of Christian work.—

Matt. xxviii. 19, 20 ; xxvi. 26–28, with 1 Cor. xi. ; Acts ii. 41, 42 ; Rom. xii. 4, 5, &c. ; 1 Cor. i. 2–10 ; xii. 12, &c. ; Ephes. i. 1 ; ii. 19–22 ; Phil. i. 1–11 ; iv. 1–3 ; 1 Thess. i. to end ; ii. 13, 14.

THE MEMBERS OF A CHRISTIAN CHURCH

Are persons admitted to fellowship, on a credible profession of personal faith in Christ, manifested by a willingness to obey His commands.

All such Members are bound to maintain the peace and order of the Society ; to promote mutual edification and encouragement ; to co-operate for the support and diffusion of the Gospel ; and to addict themselves to works of Christian benevolence and usefulness.

Any of them who act inconsistently with their profession, should be exhorted and admonished.   If any of them deny the faith, cause divisions, act immorally, or refuse subjection to the rules of Christian fellowship, they are to be excluded from the Society; and any person thus excluded is to be re-admitted upon giving satisfactory evidence of contrition and amendment.

Acts ii. 41–47; ix. 27, 28; xi. 19–24; 1 Thess. v. 14; 1 Tim. v. 20; 2 Tim. iii. 1–5; Titus iii. 10; 1 John i. 1–7; Rom. xiv.; xv. 1–7; xvi. 17; 1 Cor. v. 1 to end; xi. 16; 2 Cor. ii. 5–11; Gal. vi. 1, 2 : Col. iii. 12, 13; Ephes. iv. 2, 3,16 to end.

THE OFFICERS OF A CHRISTIAN CHURCH

Are *Bishops*, called also Elders, Pastors, and Teachers; who are to rule and instruct the Society; to expound the Word of God; to conduct Public Worship; to administer Christian Ordinances; to preside in the assemblies of the Church; to enforce the laws of Christ in its Government and discipline; and to take a general oversight of the Church and all its proceedings, "watching for souls, as those who must give account."

Also *Deacons*, who are appointed to execute the pecuniary affairs of the fellowship, under the sanction of the Pastors, and so as to relieve *them* from attending to the details of the Church's benefactions and financial concerns.

The Bishops and Deacons are to be chosen by the Church, on account of their piety, intelligence, and general qualifications for the duties of their respective offices, as indicated in the Word of God. The number of each to be decided by circumstances.

Ephes. iv. 11, &c.; Phil. i. 1; 1 Thess. v. 12; 1 Tim. iii.; v. 17; Heb. xiii. 17; 1 Peter v. 1–5; Acts vi. 1–6; Titus i. 7-9; Acts xiv. 23; xx. 17–28; 2 Cor. viii. 18, 19.

NOTE.—The word rendered "ORDAINED" in Acts xiv. 23 is

rendered " CHOSEN " in 2 Cor. viii. 19 ; and in the Old English translations by Tyndal and Cranmer, and also in the Genevan edition, it is rendered " ORDAINED BY ELECTION." The clause in 2 Cor. viii. 19 is also rendered " ordained of Churches,"— " chosen of the Congregations,"—" chosen by election of the Churches,"—" ordained of the Churches,"—in all the early English translations, from that of Wycliff ; thus showing that the Officers of a Christian Church, should be " CHOSEN " by the Church itself.—(See *Bagster's* " Hexapla.")

An " order of priests," and a clerical hierarchy, which have usurped authority in Christendom, can find no sanction in the Word of God.

Connected with Churches, as their agents and representatives,—but not as Officers in their internal organization,—are *Evangelists or Missionaries*, whose province is to preach the Gospel, and form new Churches, of Christian converts.

Acts xiii. 1-6 ; Ephes. iv. 11 ; 2 Tim. iv. 5 ; Titus i. 5.

THE ORDER AND DISCIPLINE OF A CHRISTIAN CHURCH

Should be maintained by the Society itself, through its own Officers, independently of any foreign control, political or ecclesiastical; though it is important, on grave questions, and matters of public interest, to obtain the sympathy and advisory counsel of neighbour Churches. A Church should exercise disciplinary authority, simply as the executive of the laws of Christ. The Word of God, applied with Christian candour and common sense, should supply its canons, its charter, and its code. Instruction, admonition, and discipline are its only means of administration, and weapons of power. EXCOMMUNICATION—which is simply exclusion from its own fellowship,—is its extreme and final act of discipline, to be employed only as an act of allegiance to Christ, for preserving the purity of the

Church. The excommunicated should be the objects of its faithful and tender solicitude, that discipline and instruction may be blessed to their recovery; and the restoration of penitents should always be regarded as its pleasing duty, to be discharged in brotherly love.

As no rituals or rules of Ecclesiastical uniformity, possess authority from Christ or Apostolic sanction, Pastors are free to adopt such plans and arrangements in their respective Churches, as they consider most conducive to edification and in harmony with Scripture.

The consent of the brotherhood, is the only authority necessary for by-laws and incidental regulations.

Internally, a Church requires only the practical adoption of Divine law; externally, it requires only liberty and social rights.

Acts vi. 2-5; 1 Cor. v. 4-12; xi. 2-16 to end; xii. 13, 14; 2 Cor. ii. 1-11; vi. 14 to end; Matt. xviii. 15-18; xxii. 21; Col. i. 18; ii. 16-22; 2 Tim. i. 13; ii. 2-24, 25; iii. 16, 17; Heb. iii. 6-13; Rev. xxii. 18, 19; Ephes. iv. 15, 16-32; 1 Thess. iii. 12, 13; 2 Thess. i. 1-12; ii. 15, &c.; iii. 1, 2, 6-16.

THE PECUNIARY RESOURCES AND EXPENSES OF A CHRISTIAN CHURCH

Should be provided by voluntary contributions only; no species of compulsory taxation being admissible for the support of Christianity. The Members of a Christian Church should give liberally of their own substance according to their means, and they should urge the motives of the Gospel on others, to induce them to contribute freely, to the support of the Christian Ministry and of Public Worship, for works of Charity and for the extension of the Gospel in the world. Christianity provides in this, as in other things, for all varieties of social circumstances, and for the individual action of conscience, according to means and opportunities; but the simplest and most effective mode is, by *weekly contributions, as each person can afford*, according to the apostolic rule.

Luke x. 7; Acts iv. 32, &c.; xi. 29, 30; Rom. xv. 26, 27; 1 Cor. ix. 14; xvi. 1, 2; 2 Cor. viii.; ix.; Gal. vi. 6, 10; Phil. iv. 15–19; 1 Tim. v. 17, 18, vi. 17, 18.

THE UNION OF CHRISTIAN CHURCHES

Is most desirable and advantageous, as tending to awaken Christian sympathy, to promote a spirit of Scriptural Catholicity, and to secure co-operation in Missionary efforts and other works of usefulness. While Christian affection, friendly intercourse, and holy communion, should embrace all the Churches of the Saints, yet local associations are most efficient for practical purposes; but such associations should never become Ecclesiastical Courts, or assume any coercive authority regarding the internal affairs of the several Churches affiliated. In all their united engagements they should recognise the fraternal relations of all true Christians, and maintain, inviolable, the rights of conscience and Christian liberty, and the integrity and independence of individual Churches, according to the will of Christ.

The fraternal relation of all true Christians, is the true basis of Church fellowship.

Churches should hold communion with each other, as individuals hold membership in Churches, upon the mutual recognition of true piety and in the faith of fundamental truths. Soundness of doctrine and purity of communion, are, therefore, necessary, not only to the spiritual prosperity of every Church, but also to the harmony and profitable intercourse of associated Churches. This intercourse should take place, not by constraint of human law, or by the adoption of any sectarian badges or rules of outward uniformity; but by the free exercise of holy sympathy and brotherly love.

Every Christian Church ought to be a Missionary Society to the extent of its ability. All Christian Churches ought to manifest their fellowship in the faith, by uniting in Missionary labours, and all Missionary Societies ought to be the representatives and recognised agents of affiliated Churches, which have freely united for their organisation, direction, and support.

All Christian Churches should freely receive each other's members, as brethren, and joyfully co-operate, in Scriptural efforts, for mutual edification, and for the conversion of the world to Christ.

John xvii. ; Acts xi. 19 to end ; xv. 3, 4, 22, &c. ; xviii. 27 ; xxi. 15–20 ; xxviii. 14, 15, 30, 31 ; Rom. xvi. 1, 5, 6, 7, 14, 15, 16 ; 1 Cor. i. ; 2 Cor. viii. ; ix. ; x. ; Gal. ii. ; vi. 2, 10 16 ; Ephes. vi. 18 ; Col. i. 3, 4 ; iv. 7 to end ; 1 Thess. i. ; Rev. i. ; iii. 22 ; xxii. 17:

SUMMARY.

In considering the above outline, it should be premised, that those who are distinguished by the maintenance of these principles, hold, also, the general doctrines of the Christian faith, in harmony with all Protestant bodies, generally designated "Evangelical." They maintain the Divine inspiration and authority of the sacred Scriptures; the Eternity, Independence, Sovereignty, Omnipotence, Omniscience, Holiness, Justice, and Benevolence of God; the depravity of human nature; the responsibility and guilt of mankind; the revelation of mercy and Salvation by the Gospel; the necessity of repentance and conversion; the Divinity, Atonement, and Mediation of the Lord Jesus Christ; the Sovereign efficacy of Divine grace, and Justification by Faith; the personality of the Holy Spirit, and His agency in conversion and sanctification; the necessity of personal holiness and good works, as fruits and evidences of justifying faith; the glorious hope of immortality; the certainty of future judgment; the sufferings of the wicked; and the happiness of the righteous.

CONGREGATIONAL INDEPENDENCY *is not an embodiment of sectarian peculiarities.* It is THE RENUNCIATION OF SECTARIANISM, IN FAVOUR OF CHRISTIANITY. It expresses, not the whims and inventions of man, but the will and ordinances of

God; not the reckless insubordination of fanaticism, but the humble obedience of faith.

Its spirit is, not schismatical strife among Christians : but undivided allegiance to Christ.

It is a claim and an effort to revive and practise New Testament Christianity.

While it is, in common with other forms of Protestantism. distinguished from State Establishments, by the negative designations of " Nonconformity" and " Dissent," its direct and positive tendency, is, *to develop the true spirit of* THE REFORMATION.

Its chief requirements are, the recognition of Divine authority, personal piety, simplicity and spirituality in worship, religious liberty, and Christian union.

It is not Denominationalism. It is the proper antidote and true antagonist of sectarian intolerance, bigotry, and exclusiveness.

Just as, in general Society, the family or the nation is distinct and independent, and *therefore* free to make friendly alliances with other families or with other nations. discreetly, and in he mutual exercise of affection and respect,—so all Christian persons and all Christian Churches, *according to New Testament Independency*, should unite and co-operate with all whom they regard as "sound in the faith of the Gospel, holding the head, even Christ." Neither should they be separated from " the communion of saints," by any denominational or sectarian peculiarities, nor ecclesiastically united, in pretence, by any yoke of bondage, with those whom they believe to be separated from Christ, living in sin, or holding pernicious errors.

Evangelical Congregational Independency, unites with the true Protestantism of a Scriptural faith, the true catholicity of a universal Christian brotherhood.

It maintains the strictest loyalty to truth and the largest exercise of charity.

Its distinctive elements are, " the love of the brotherhood " and THE SUPREMACY OF CHRIST.

All who hold these principles are sacredly bound to honour and practise them, rejoicing in Christian liberty, cherishing and manifesting Christian love, " as free, and not using liberty as a cloak of maliciousness, but as the servants of God."

They " should earnestly contend for the faith which was once delivered to the saints ; " and, believing that " CHRIST IS THE HEAD OF THE CHURCH," as " He is the Saviour of the Body," they are pledged to uphold the honours of His Crown, while they glory in His Cross.

Members of Independent Evangelical Churches are pre-eminently required to be " living epistles of Christ, " manifesting in all things the spirit of the Gospel, and " endeavouring to keep the unity of the Spirit in the bond of peace."

They should commend New Testament Church principles to other Christians, not as topics of sectarian controversy, but as ordinances of Christ. They should kindly and charitably bear with the prejudices and unscriptural notions which still prevail among members of various Evangelical communities; carefully avoiding all bitterness and bigotry, while endeavouring to expound to them the way of God more perfectly. As Non-conformists they should be careful, to present these truths, to pious members of our National Establishment, *not as denominational peculiarities*, not in a turbulent or defiant spirit, but with the holy earnestness of Christian affection, and for the honour of Christ, in the union and edification of His Church.

Remembering that some of the aspects of " Dissent " have been very repulsive to " Established Church " men, and that the abuses of Independency and the inconsistencies of its professors, always furnish its opponents with their most plausible arguments against it, they should humbly and prayerfully consider their own solemn responsibilities, while recommending the "more excellent way" of Divine Institutions, to fellow-Christians, who still adhere to doctrines and commandments of men. Having no yoke of canon laws or carnal ordinances, to hinder or hamper the exercise of their Christian sympathies, and having no ecclesiastical machinery to suppress or supersede Christian devotedness, they are the more free to unite with all whom they love in the Truth, and the more distinctly pledged, by profession and consistency, to live and labour for the salvation of sinners and for the instruction and help of fellow-believers. If they be slothful selfish sectaries—as their system cannot be blamed—the guilt must rest entirely upon themselves.

They should delight to maintain fraternal intercourse with fellow-Christians of every name, and practically to aid them in every "work of faith and labour of love."

In the words of one of the most eminent and beloved of those who have lately seceded from the Establishment,* because of conscientious attachment to these principles, it may be said that those who enjoy this Christian liberty for themselves are bound to unite heart and voice to secure its blessings for others :—

"Uniting with all who love the Redeemer they should recognise with gratitude every work of the Spirit *within* the Establishment *as well as without* it ; and with much prayer, with constant dependence on the Holy Spirit, with a supreme desire to glorify God, and with an abundant exercise of faith, hope, and love, they should persevere in their efforts, till the blessing of God renders their triumph a decisive step towards the Evangelisation of the world."

Sacredly maintaining the rights of conscience for all, study-

* Hon. and Rev. Baptist W. Noel. 1858.

ing to promote the general well-being of society, rendering due obedience to the laws, and praying for kings and all that are in authority, they should ever remember that their "citizenship is in heaven." They are "called with a holy calling" to promote "glory to God in the highest, and on earth peace, good-will towards men," while the bond and motto of their religious fellowship, should always be, "GRACE BE WITH ALL THEM THAT LOVE OUR LORD JESUS CHRIST IN SINCERITY. AMEN."

APPENDIX.

———•———

Though truth rests not on human authority, and it is an essential principle of New Testament Christianity, that our "faith should not stand in the wisdom of men, but in the power of God" (1 Cor. ii. 5) ; yet it may be interesting and useful to peruse the following testimonies, selected from various writers of eminence, regarding the Scriptural constitution of Christian Churches.

CHURCHES, CHURCH OFFICERS, &c.

"A visible Church * of Christ is *a congregation* of faithful men, in which the pure Word of God is preached," &c.— Nineteenth Article, English Book of Common Prayer.

"The term Εχχλησια in the New Testament (and by the ancient Fathers) primarily denoted *an assembly of Christians;* *i.e.*, of believers in the Christian religion, in distinction from all others."—*Coleman's* " Christian Antiquities" (from Augusti, Neander, Munter, Rheinwald, &c.), p. 26.

" The Churches to which the Apostolic Epistles were written, *were select companies*, each adult of which had been admitted into the Church, on an intelligent profession of faith, such as approved itself to the Apostles and their coadjutors;

* "*A Church* is the correct rendering.—See *Archbishop Whately's* "Kingdom of Christ," p. 150, &c.

and when any individual acted inconsistently with his profession, he was *excluded* from the company, till he gave satisfactory evidence of true repentance."—*Rev. T. Scott,* " Commentary on 1 Tim."

Let us now consider what a Church is. A Church, then, I take to be a voluntary society of men, joining themselves together of their own accord, in order to the public worshiping of God, in such a manner as they judge acceptable to Him and effectual to the salvation of their souls. I say it is a free and voluntary society. Nobody is born a member of any Church ; otherwise the religion of parents would descend unto children, by the same right of inheritance as their temporal estates, and every one would hold his faith by the same tenure that he does his lands, than which nothing can be more absurd."—*Locke,* " Letter concerning Toleration."

" The new Churches out of Palestine, formed themselves after the pattern of the mother Church in Jerusalem. Their presidents were the elders (πρεσβυτεροι, Επισκοποι), *officially of equal rank;* although, in many Churches, individuals among them had a personal authority over others. Under the superintendence of these elders were the *deacons and deaconesses.*—*Gieseler,* " Eccles. Hist.," i. 88, &c.

" The bishops and priests," or presbyters, that is, " elders," " were at one time, and were no two things, but both one office in the beginning of Christ's religion." " The people, before Christian princes were, commonly did elect their bishops and priests."—*Archbishop Cranmer;* " Burnet's History of the Reformation," vol. ii. ; Records, pp. 97, 98.

" By divers arguments from Scripture, he (*Jerome*) proves that bishop and presbyter are one and the same. Acts 20, They who, v. 17, are called *presbyters,* are v. 28, called *bishops.* Titus i. 5, *He left him to ordain elders,* and v. 7, it is added, *for a bishop,* &c. Whence he infers that "bishop" and "presbyter" are one and the same. As also Phil. i. the Apostle writes only to bishops and deacons. And 1 Tim. iii. he gives the rules only to bishops and deacons, &c.—*Bishop Burnet,* "Observations on the First Canon."

"The same persons are in this chapter called ' elders,' or *presbyters,* ' and overseers or *bishops* ' (28 v. Greek); it must therefore be allowed, that these were not distinct orders of ministers in the Church at that time. Every impartial man must allow that, if Timothy had been at this time bishop of Ephesus, in that sense for which some contend, the Apostles would have given these elders some exhortation to pay proper deference to his episcopal authority." "The deacons were primarily appointed to dispense the charity of the Church, and to manage its secular concerns."—*Rev. T. Scott,* "Commentary on Acts xx. 17," &c.

"The English Version has hardly dealt fairly, in this case, with the Sacred Text, in rendering *episkopous,* ver. 28, ' overseers;' whereas it ought there, as in all other places, to have been ' *bishops,*' that the fact of *elders and bishops, having been originally and apostolically synonymous, might be apparent to the ordinary English reader, which now it is not.*"—*Rev. H. Alford, Dean of Canterbury* (Greek Testament) on Acts xx. 17, &c.

"In the primitive state of the Church" "Christian Churches were founded in distant places, as the Apostles did find opportunity or received direction to found them, which, therefore could not, without extreme inconvenience, have resort or reference to one authority anywhere fixed. Each Church, therefore, separately, did order its own affairs, without recourse to others, except for charitable advice or relief in cases of extraordinary difficulty or urgent need. Each Church was endowed with a perfect liberty and a full authority, without dependence or subordination to others, to govern its own members, to manage its own affairs, to decide controversies and causes incident among themselves, without allowing appeals, or rendering accounts to others. This appeareth by the apostolical writings of St. Paul and St. John, to single Churches, wherein they are supposed able to exercise spiritual power for establishing decency, removing disorders, correcting offences, deciding causes," &c.

"The ancients did assert to each bishop a free, absolute, independent authority, subject to none, directed by none, accountable to none, on earth, in the administration of affairs properly concerning his particular Church."—*Rev. Isaac Barrow, D.D.*—**Works, vol vii.**

"The power of enacting laws, of appointing teachers and ministers, and determining controversies, was lodged in the people at large; nor did the Apostles, although vested with Divine authority, either resolve on or sanction anything, without the concurrence of the general body of Christians, of which the Church was composed. There can be no doubt that the Apostles might have filled up a vacancy in their own number without any reference to the multitude; yet we find them convoking the general body of Christians, to take share in this matter. When the seven men were to be appointed the whole affair was, we see, submitted by the Apostles to the judgment of the Church at large. When a question arose at Antioch, respecting the authority of the law of Moses (Acts xv.), the Apostles, inasmuch as they were constituted by Christ Himself expounders of the Divine will, might, with the greatest reason, have taken the cognisance and determination thereof to themselves; yet we find them here again convoking and taking counsel with the whole Church. I conceive it to be unnecessary, or otherwise it would be easy to point out several passages in St. Paul's Epistles which lead to the same inference with the above." "When the voice of the multitude, in the election of any one, to the sacred ministry, was unanimous, it was considered in the light of a Divine call. In compliance with the express commands of our Lord himself and his Apostles, those teachers and ministers of the Church were, from the first, maintained and supplied with every neccessary by the people, for whose edification they laboured."

"Although all the Churches were, in the first age of Christianity, united together in one common bond of faith and love, and were in every respect ready to promote the interests and welfare of each other, by a reciprocal interchange of good offices; yet, with regard to government and internal economy, every individnal Church considered itself as an independent community, none of them ever looking beyond the circle of its own members for assistance or recognising any sort of external influence or authority."—*Mosheim's* "Commentaries on the Affairs of Christians;" *Vidal's* Translation, vol. i. p. 203, &c.

"The ancient dioceses are never said to contain *Churches* in the plural, but only ' a Church ' in the singular. . . . As for the word *diocese*, by which the bishop's flock is usually expressed, I do not remember that ever I found it used in this sense by any of the ancients; but there is another word, still retained by us, by which they frequently denominated the bishop's cure, and that is ' parish,' . . . by that term denoting the very same that we now call a parish—viz., a competent number of Christians, dwelling near together, having but one bishop, pastor, or minister set over them, with whom they all met at one time, to worship and serve God. . . . A parish and a particular church are synonymous terms, signifying one and the same thing; and consequently a bishop, having but one parish under his jurisdiction, could extend his government no farther than one single congregation, because a single congregation and parish were all one, of the same bulk and magnitude." . . . "All the people *of a diocese* did, every Sunday, meet all together in one place, to celebrate Divine Service." . . . "When the bishop of a Church was dead, all the people of that Church met together in one place to choose a new bishop." . . . "It is expressly said by the ancients that there were but two distinct ecclesiastical orders, —viz., 'bishops and deacons' or 'presbyters and deacons.'"

"The original institution of the deacons, as in Acts vi., was *to serve tables*, which includes these two things,—a looking after the poor, and attendance at the Lord's table."—*Lord Chancellor King* "On the Constitution, &c., of the Primitive Church, within the first 300 years after Christ," chap. ii. &c.

"One single passage from the apostolical writings has not yet been produced, in which it appears from the context, that the two terms 'presbuteros' and 'episkopos' (presbyter or elder, and bishop) mean different offices. Nay, we can say more than this, which may be called a negative and presumptive proof only,—that there is the strongest positive evidence which the nature of the thing can admit, that in those writings, the two terms *uniformly* mean the same office. The Apostle Paul, in the directions he gave to Timothy about the proper supply of Churches with suitable ministers, takes particular notice of two orders and no more. One of them he calls bishops and the other deacons, &c.

"In any intermediate sense, between a single congregation and the whole community of Christians, not one instance can be brought, of the application of the word (*Church*) in Sacred Writ. We speak now, indeed (and this has been the manner of ages) of the Gallican Church, the Greek Church, the Church of England, the Church of Scotland, as of societies independent and complete in themselves. Such a phraseology was never adopted in the days of the Apostles. They did not say the Church of Asia, or the Church of Macedonia, or the Church of Achaia. The plural number is invariably used when more congregations than one are spoken of, unless the subject be of the whole commonwealth of Christ. Nor is this the manner of the penmen of Sacred Writ only. It is the constant usage of the term in the writings of ecclesiastical authors for the two first centuries," &c. — *Professor Campbell,* "Lectures on Ecclesiastical History," vol. 1, pp. 128, 204, 205, &c.

"The Christian Church (ἡ ἐχχλησία Τοῦ Χριστοῦ) is a religious, moral society, connected together by a common faith in Christ, and which seeks to represent, in its united life, 'the Kingdom of God,' announced by Christ. . . . Differences relating to the objects of Christian faith and ecclesiastical life, early separated the Church into various distinct societies, each of which commonly assumed to itself exclusively the name of 'the true Church of Christ,' and branded the others with the titles of 'heresy and schism.'"

"While the old unreformed Church associations (Eastern and Western) are continually prejudiced by this *particularism,* Protestants, on the contrary, acknowledge every ecclesiastical society, which holds Christian truth, in greater or less purity and clearness, to be a preparatory institution for the Kingdom of God, and, as such, belonging to *the universal Christian Church,* whose true essence is the invisible Church, the entire number of all true believers, throughout the world."—*Geiseler,* "Ecclesiastical History, Introduction," pp. 1, 2.

"The earliest Fathers follow the Scriptures, in speaking of the Church *in* a place.

"The earliest ecclesiastical epistle extant was from 'the Church of God which sojourneth at Rome' to 'the Church of God which sojourneth at Corinth.'" *Ignatius, Polycarp,* and *Origen* speak of "the Church in Athens," "the Church in Alexandria," &c.—*Bennett's* "Theology of the Early Christian Church," p. 198.

" The first use of the term ' Catholic ' exhibits a Congregational Church. ' Wherever the bishop appears, there let the multitude be; as wherever Jesus Christ may be, there is the Catholic Church.' "—*Ignatius ad Smyrn.* c. 8. Ibid.

CHURCH AND STATE.

" The civil magistrate being become protector of the Church and, consequently, supreme HEAD and director of it, *the ministry is mostly in his power :* that mutual dependency between the clergy and the people being, by means of a settled revenue, quite broken and destroyed."

" While a Church is *in its natural state* of INDEPENDENCY, it is not in his (the civil ruler's) power to improve those conjunctures to the advantage of the State, by a proper application of religion, but when the alliance is made (between the Church and State), and, *consequently the Church is under his direction,* he hath then authority to prescribe such exercises of religion," &c.—*Bishop Warburton.*

" The end is, the protection and support of true religion. But the civil magistrate who is to establish it, assuming to himself the sole authority of judging which is so, *must necessarily conclude in favour of his own :* so that the established religion, all over the world, will be the magistrate's: that *is, for one place where the true religion is established, the false will be established in a thousand.*

" The care of souls cannot belong to the civil magistrate, because his power consists only in outward force ; but true and saving religion consists in the inward persuasion of the mind, without which nothing can be acceptable to God. And such is the nature of the understanding, that it cannot be compelled to the belief of anything by outward force," &c.

" The care of the salvation of men's souls cannot belong to

the magistrates, because, though the rigour of laws and the force of penalties were capable to convince and change men's minds, yet would not that help at all to the salvation of their souls."—" In the variety and contradictions of opinions in religion, wherein the princes of the world are as much divided as in their secular interests, the narrow way would be much straightened ; one country alone would be in the right, and all the rest of the world put under an obligation of following their princes, in the way that leads to destruction," &c.—*Locke*.

" When the Roman Empire became Christian, when a Christian Emperor bore *the sword*, . . . when relieved from the terrors of Pagan persecutions the Christians became possessed of civil power, their animosity increased. Worldly prosperity is corruptive, and instead of more halcyon days of peace and happiness, which the Church promised to itself from the acquisition of power, history is sure to date from this period its degeneracy and corruption. . . . The history of this period, faithfully related, informs us, that although the Christian Church was delivered from persecution and advanced in worldly consideration and power, yet did it acquire no *real* accession of worth, dignity, or exaltation, by its connection with the Imperial throne. Nay, from that very time its degeneracy and corruption are most indubitably to be dated. From that period worldly power and riches became the object of its leaders; not purity and virtue. Many entered the Christian Church, and obtained its honours and dignities, by base dissimulation of their principles, to please the Emperor, and recommend themselves to his favour. And the consequent extension of the Christian religion, among the Heathen nations, was, as Mosheim observes, *in name, not in reality.* . . . This grand enemy of the Christian Church, the devil, had begun his attack upon her, first by the terrors of persecution. He failed in this attempt: the blood of the martyrs became the seed of the Church. He then changed his mode of operation. He beguiled the Christians with the promise of worldly power and splendour : and it was from this successful mode of corruption that he was at length enabled to produce *Antichrist.*"—*Archdeacon Woodhouse* on " The Apocalypse," pp. 138, 191, 192.

" I should hope that it must appear to every considerate reader, that a *National Establishment* is one thing, and a *Christian Church* another."—*Archdeacon Daubeny.*

" Neither our Lord nor His Apostles enjoined a National Religious Establishment."—*Chancellor Dealtry.*

" The Union of the Church with the State has entirely obscured and hidden from the world, the liberality with which devout and pious Anglicans would, in obedience to Christ's commands, maintain their Pastors ; because their present payments are made under compulsion of law. Five thousand Pastors, maintained by the zeal and generosity of the Churches, would be an impressive proof of faith and love ; but sixteen thousand maintained by compulsion of law, are no proof of faith and love, whatsoever." . . . " Upon the removal of the union the different denominations in England, as the different denominations in the United States, would act in harmony, to the great improvement of the Churches and to the comfort of the country at large,"

" It is the will of Christ, as manifested in the New Testament, that each Church should select its own Pastor, with careful regard to the pastoral qualifications required by him; but the Anglican Churches allow strangers to choose their Pastors for them ; and receive multitudes of *unconverted Pastors,* because the State has given to Patrons the right to nominate them." . . . " As the Churches have relinquished their own right of nominating their Pastors, they have likewise neglected to maintain Christ's rights over them. The

Church of real believers is the House of Christ, *over which* HE ALONE HAS THE RIGHT TO RULE. But the Anglican Churches have allowed the State to usurp His authority. . . . By this faithless consent to transfer to the State, the authority of Christ, the Churches necessarily submit to a disgraceful neglect or desecration of the ordinances of their Lord."

"The union of the Church with the State is corrupt an unscriptural in its principles; its influence upon various classes of men is noxious; it injures various great interests of the country; it maintains corruption in doctrine; it has ruined Church discipline; it hinders the evangelization of the country; it perpetuates schisms in the Churches; it renders the reformation of the Establishment impossible; it impedes the progress of religion; it embarrasses the Government; and *it lends strength to all the Papal Establishments of Europe.*"

"All history proclaims, that the union between Churches and Governments, tried through long centuries of misrule, and found everywhere to be only potent for evil, *should at length give place to* CHRIST'S OWN LAW OF SPIRITUAL LIBERTY, *through which alone* His Churches can accomplish their beneficent mission, to bring the nations of the earth into the service of the Redeemer, and to make all intellects and all hearts tributary to His glory."—*Hon. and Rev. B. W. Noel,* "Essay on Union of Church and State," pp. 89, 304, 325.

"It appears to me, that in this colony, we are placed in a peculiarly favourable position, for considering our Church relations, *because one great rock of offence has been taken out of the way*—I mean the connection between Church and State. We can approach the matters in dispute, simply as questions of Evangelical truth and Christian expediency. Neither social, nor civil, nor ecclesiastical distinctions, interfere to distract our view or irritate our feelings."—*Bishop of Adelaide,* "Letter to the Rev. T. Binney."

" Primitive Christianity went forth without arms, or patronage, or wealth, ' taking nothing of the Gentiles ' but what the Gentiles willingly gave, and established itself in the earth, not by the force of legislation, but by the grace of God.

" *By removing religion from the jurisdiction of the civil power, and resting it, for support and promulgation, on the arm of God and the voluntary zeal of its friends, we clear it from all suspicion, and, by maintaining its spiritual purity, increase its general efficiency.* The character of Christianity, as much so as that of its individual followers, is of infinite consequence to its moral influence. It must stand clear from the suspicion of being the tool of princes, or the trade of priests; but how can this ever be the case, at least in the estimation of multitudes, so long as it is seen in alliance with the State?"—*Rev. John Angel James.*

IMPARTIAL TESTIMONIALS.

" The Independents, properly so-called, conceiving that they could draw from Scripture alone that form of ecclesiastical policy which was most consonant to the spirit of Christianity, rejected tradition, as the basis of the various usurpations, whether by the Pope, the Greek Patriarch, by Laud, or others, which had tyrannized over and disgraced Christian society. Their form of ecclesiastical government was especially simple. That each congregation, as a complete Church within itself, should have full power to elect its own pastor and office-bearers, and manage all its own affairs, without the control of prelates, or of presbyteries, synods, and assemblies, or, in short, any other ecclesiastical institution; though they held that every Church should cultivate a communion with others of whose principles and practice it approved; and they admitted the use, while they denied the jurisdiction, of classical assemblies. In no material point of doctrine did they differ from the Presbyterians. The number of this sect, in its strictest definition, was limited; though it included men of great learning and many of high rank."

"The grand principle by which the Independents surpassed all other sects, was universal toleration to all denominations of Christians, whose religion was not conceived to be hostile to the peace of the State—a principle to which they were faithful in the height of power, as well as under persecution. In this, for which they were bitterly reviled by the Presbyterians, they set an example to Christendom."—*Brodie*, "History of the British Empire," vol. iii. pp. 501, 506.

"The Independents—that body much to be respected indeed for their numbers, but far more to be held in lasting veneration, for the unshaken fortitude in which, at all times, they have maintained their attachment to civil and religious liberty, and holding fast by their principles, have carried to its utmost pitch the great doctrine of absolute toleration—men to whose ancestors this country will ever acknowledge a boundless debt of gratitude as long as freedom is prized among us; for they, I fearlessly confess it, they—with whatever *ridicule* some may visit their excesses, or with whatever *blame* others—they, with the zeal of martyrs, the purity of early Christians, the skill and courage of the most renowned warriors, obtained for England the free Constitution she now enjoys."—*Lord Brougham*, Speech in the House of Commons, on Jamaican Missions.

"If we would open our eyes, we should see that we are beholden to the sober and moderate Dissenters, for the continuance of a considerable part of our theological principles among us, even those which the Church of England and the Reformers had left us. If there had been none of the party, the Church of England had been long since ruined; for if the High Churchmen had no check, they would have brought in Popery, before this time, by a side-wind, and by their over-valuing of ceremony, in Divine worship."—*Rev. John Edwards, D.D.*, "Preacher," part ii. p. 177.

"As a member and minister of the Church of Christ, I cannot be so ungrateful to the Dissenting body, as to forget their past and present services to the cause of Christianity. Many of their community have shone in their respective eras as the light and glory of the Catholic Church. No library can make any pretensions to completeness in the department of practical Divinity unless it be enriched with the works of *Hare, Owen, Edwards, Baxter, Henry, Doddridge, Watts*, and many others of scarcely inferior name. Of our most useful and popular commentaries on the entire Scriptures the greater number has proceeded from the pens of Nonconformists."— *Rev. John Ryland.*

" I cannot shut my eyes to the fact, that this Independent connection, has succeeded in maintaining, for a longer period, a more perfect uniformity of doctrine in its ministers, without a confession of faith, than any other Church with which I am acquainted, has done, with the help of such a confession."— *Rev. James Carlisle*, Minister of the Scot's Church, Dublin, "On the Use and Abuse of Creeds and Confessions of Faith."

CHRISTIAN ANTIQUITIES.

"The history of the Apostles exhibits the Church to us under two opposite aspects. Under one it introduces her as all perfection. At her birth she appears to us as the reconciliation of all earthly contradictions; as a harmonious choir hymning the praises of God with the tongues of all nations and peoples under heaven.

"The other aspect under which the Church is here depicted is equally extensive, though of a different kind. Under it the Church is represented in labour and warfare; she can call nothing her own; she has everything to win; to labour for it, and to gain it by a hard struggle. . . .

"It is the same conflict as that which the gospels open to

our eyes, in the life of our Lord. Here, too, there gleams the heavenly radiance of the majesty of the only-begotten Son of God. In the history of the early Church we have to study, not only its rest and happiness, but also its toils, its triumphs, and its conflicts.—"Apostolic History," by *Baumgarten*, vol. ii. pp. 1, 2.

Here it is instructive to glance at the earliest notices of the Christians extant in the writings of their adversaries; and, although it is out of chronological order, it may be interesting to peruse the brief records of this class, that remain to us, of their character and condition, in the age immediately succeeding that of the Apostles, even before we investigate the apostolic history and the planting of the Church. An invaluable collection, from the critical researches of German scholars, is provided for the English reader, in *Coleman's* "Christian Antiquities," from which we abridge the following:—

"Greek and Roman authors take but little notice of the early Christians. They generally regarded them with contempt or detestation, as a dangerous Jewish sect.

"Accordingly, the passages in which Suetonius, Tacitus, Arian, Antoninus, Dio Cassius, and others, speak of Christians, throw little or no light on their manners and customs.

"The most important notices of this kind occur in the letters of Pliny the Younger, who, according to the most approved chronology, was Governor of Bythynia in the years 103, 104; and in the writings of Lucian of Samosata, an opponent of Christianity, who also lived in the second century. Pliny had been instructed by the Emperor Trajan, to keep a strict guard against all secret societies, and, under this commission, proceeded to severe measures against the assemblies of Christians. In reporting his proceedings to the Emperor, he takes occasion to explain the character of these Christians, and the nature of their assembles. In this manner he unconsciously passes a high encomium upon these primitive Christians. The letter itself was written but about forty years after the death of St. Paul, and, together with Trajan's reply, constitutes the most important record, extant, of the times immediately succeeding the Apostles."

PLINY TO TRAJAN.

(PLINIUS TRAJANO.)

" *Solenne est mihi, Domine, omnia, de quibus dubito, ad Te referre*," &c.

Translation by Melmoth :—

"Having never been present at any trials concerning those who profess Christianity, I am unacquainted, not only with the nature of their crimes or the measure of their punishment, but how far it is proper to enter into an examination concerning them ; whether, therefore, any difference is usually made, with respect to the ages of the guilty, or no distinction is to be observed between the young and the adult ;—whether repentance entitles them to pardon, or, if a man has once been a Christian, it avails nothing to desist from his error ; whether the very profession of Christianity, unattended with any criminal act, or only the crimes themselves, inherent in the profession, are punishable ; on all these points, I am greatly doubtful. In the meanwhile, the method I have observed towards those who have been brought before me as Christians, is this :—I interrogated them whether they were Christians ; if they confessed, I repeated the question twice again, adding threats at the same time ; when, if they still persevered, I ordered them to be immediately punished ; for I was persuaded, whatever the nature of their opinions might be, that a contumacious and inflexible obstinacy, certainly deserved correction. There were others also brought before me, possessed with the same infatuation, but being citizens of Rome, I directed them to be carried thither. But this crime, spreading (as is usually the case), while it was actually under prosecution, several instances of the same nature occurred. An information was presented to me, without any name prescribed, containing a charge against several persons, who, upon examination, denied that they were Christians, or had ever been so. They repeated after me, an invocation to the gods, and offered religious rites, with wine and frankincense, before your statue (which for this purpose I had ordered to be brought, together with those of the gods), and even reviled the name of Christ: whereas there is no forcing, it is said, those who are really Christians, into a compliance with any of these articles; I thought proper, therefore, to discharge them. Some of those who were accused by a witness in person, at first confessed themselves Christians, but immediately after denied it; while the rest owned indeed that they had been of that number formerly, but had now (some above three, others more, and a few above twenty years ago) forsaken that error. They all worshipped your statue and the images of the gods, throwing out imprecations, at the same time, against the name of Christ. They affirmed, that the whole of their guilt or error was, that they met on a certain stated day, before it was light, and addressed themselves, in a form of prayer, to Christ, as to a God; binding themselves, by a solemn oath, not for the purposes of any wicked design, but never to commit any fraud, theft, or adultery; never to falsify their word, nor deny a trust, when they should be called upon to deliver it up; after which it was their custom to separate, and then to reassemble, to eat in common, a harmless meal. From this custom, however, they desisted after the publication of my edict, by which, according to your orders, I forbade the meeting of any assemblies. After receiving this account, I judged it so much the more necessary to endeavour to extort the real truth, by putting two female slaves to the torture, who were said to administer in their religious functions; but I could discover nothing more than an absurd and excessive superstition. I thought proper, therefore, to adjourn all further proceedings in this affair, in order to consult with you. For it appears to be a matter highly deserving your consideration; more especially, as great numbers must be involved in the danger of these prosecutions, this inquiry having already extended, and being still likely to extend, to persons of all ranks and ages, and even of both sexes. For this contagious superstition is not confined to the cities only, but has spread its infection among the country villages. Nevertheless, it still seems possible to remedy this evil and restrain its progress. The temples, at least, which were almost deserted, begin now to be frequented, and the sacred solemnities, after a long intermission, are again revived; while there is a general demand for victims, which, for some time past, have met with but few purchasers. From hence it is easy to imagine what numbers might be reclaimed from this error, if a pardon were granted to those who shall repent."

TRAJAN TO PLINY.

"The method you have pursued, my dear Pliny, in the proceedings against those Christians which were brought before you, is extremely proper; as it is not possible to lay down any fixed plan by which to act in all cases of this nature. But I would not have you officiously enter into any inquiries concerning them. If, indeed, they should be brought before you, and the crime is proved, they must be punished, with this restriction, however, that when the party denies himself to be a Christian, and shall make it evident that he is not, by invoking our gods, let him—notwithstanding any former suspicion—be pardoned upon his repentance. Informations, without the accuser's name subscribed, ought not to be received in prosecutions of any sort, as it is introducing a very dangerous precedent, and by no means agreeable to the equity of my government."

"From this record of antiquity, we learn of the early Christians,—

" 1. That they were accustomed to meet, on a certain stated day, for religious worship.

2. Their meetings were held in the morning, before daylight—doubtless that they might the better avoid the notice of their enemies.

3. They appear not to have had at this time any stated place of worship.

4. They worshipped Christ as God.

It appears that these Christians were not only acquainted with the doctrine of the Divinity of Christ, but manifested great boldness in asserting it.

5. They celebrated the sacrament and their love feasts, in these assemblies. This is implied in their binding themselves by a solemn oath not to commit sin, and in their coming together to take bread, " ad capiendum cibum promiscuum tamen et innoxium." These religious rites appear also to have been accompanied with the reading and exposition of the Scriptures : it seems to be included in these solemnities, though it is not distinctly mentioned.

6. This epistle bears honourable testimony to unflinching stedfastness of faith in these Christians, which Pliny styles ' an absurd and excessive superstition.'

7. This epistle affords a striking proof of the early and extensive propagation of Christianity, and of its tendency to overthrow idolatry."

LUCIAN.

" Lucian of Samosata travelled in Syria, Asia Minor, Italy, and France, and had the best means of becoming acquainted with the Christians, who had already become numerous in those countries. From his frequent and reproachful mention of the Christians of his day, we may collect the following particulars :—

" 1. He speaks of the followers of Christ, by their appropriate name, 'Christians,' though in speaking of them, he usually employs some reproachful epithet.

2. He speaks of the Author of this religion, as one who lived in Palestine, and was crucified. He styles him a great man, and says that his followers reverence him, as their law-giver.

3. He particularly mentions the *fraternity* of Christians, their denial of the gods of the Greeks, and their worshipping him crucified.

4. He records their readiness to relieve and to support those who were sick or in prison.

5. He mentions their δεῖπνα ποικίλα, their manifold meals, referring obviously to their *agapæ* and sacramental suppers. . .

6. It is observable also that Lucian makes mention of the sacred books of the Christians : and also,

7. Of their community of goods, as is described, Acts iv. 32–37 ; and,

Finally, of certain prohibited articles, as by the Church at Jerusalem, they were required to abstain from things strangled, and from blood ; all which evinces their piety and benevolence, and diligence in the Christian life." *

Returning, from these imperfect but very important frag-ments of Heathen testimony, we may, with special interest, pursue the records of apostolic labour, and study the distinctive features of the primitive Christian communities.

"The professors of the Christian religion were originally denominated ' Saints ' (ἅγιοι). This is their usual appellation in Sacred Scripture ; and it is applied, not only to apostles and teachers, but generally, to the community of Christians.

"'The various names which Christians had assumed for themselves, as ' disciples,' ' believers,' ' brethren,' and the like, ultimately gave place to one, which soon gained ascendancy

* *Coleman's* " Christian Antiquities," pp. 17–19.

among friends and foes, and supplanted all others. From the
first they refused all sectarian names. They would call no
man 'Master,' neither would they receive any title which
should imply that their religion was of human origin.

"Providentially a name was conferred on them, of which
we have a distinct account in the eleventh chapter of the Acts
of the Apostles.

"The form of this word, Χριστιανοί, clearly proves it to be
a Latin derivative from the Greek Χριστος, Christ.

"On the supposition that the Pagan inhabitants of Antioch,
in derision, first promulgated this name as a nickname, it is
easy to see how it might come into general use among the
Romans. The Roman historians generally regarded the Christians as an insignificant and contemptible faction. Tacitus
says, 'Nero inflicted the severest punishments on those who
were commonly denominated "Christians," and were detested
for their crimes. Their name they derived from one *Christus*,
who, in the reign of Tiberius, suffered under Pontius Pilate.'
Suetonius, also, evidently referring to Christians, relates that
Jews were expelled from Rome because of their ceaseless
tumults, to which they were instigated by one named
Chrestus."

"It would seem that the Apostles adopted the name which
had been imposed upon them in derision, and rejoiced to bear
this reproach. From the Apostles their followers adopted it as
the exclusive name of their body. To be denominated "a
Christian" was, in the estimation of professors and martyrs,
their highest honour. . . .

"It was a favourite sentiment with the primitive Christians,
that the name of *Christian* would be sufficient to prevent all
sectarian divisions, and to preserve and perpetuate among them
unity of faith and doctrine."

"I honour Peter," said Gregory of Nazianzen; "but I am

not called by his name. I honour Paul; but I am not of Paul. The name I bear is not derived of man; but I am of God." "No sect or Church took their name from the Apostles," observes Epiphanius. "We have not heard of the followers of Peter, Paul, Bartholomew, or Thaddeus. But all the Apostles from the beginning held one faith, and preached, not themselves, but JESUS CHRIST their Lord."

"*For this reason they gave all the Churches one name*, derived, not from themselves, but from their Lord Jesus Christ, after they had begun to be called 'Christians' at Antioch.

"As they all had 'one Lord,' so were they also *one*, and bore the common name of Christians, professing themselves to be the followers of Him, *not as the head of their sect or party*, but as the author of their common faith.

"*They even refused the name of Christ's Church*, claiming to be only A CHRISTIAN CHURCH, *i.e.*, a body of Christians." *

"In the history of the origin of the Christian Church three representations are given of it.

"The first is coincident with the historical foundation and establishment of the Church. The community of the first-fruits united in brotherly fellowship, and, meeting together in a single house, appears as that spiritual unity which combines in one organization of Divine life, all the varieties of the human race under heaven.

"The second exhibition of the Church in the times of the Apostles is the great assembly at Jerusalem. In it the representatives of the Gentile Churches confer with those of the Jewish Church, and they, together, come to a unanimous resolution concerning the future development of the Church in all nations.

"The third representation of the Universal Church is that which is now, in prospect, placed before us.

* *Coleman's* "Christian Antiquities," pp. 23, 24.

"In consequence of that decisive resolution the conversion of the heathen has gone on to a great extent, and has begun to embrace the whole world."

"THE FIRST CHURCH OF THE GENTILES

arose in Antioch, but *no Apostle was present or took part in founding it.* Its very institution cannot record the name of its author. And it is from this community that the mission is sent forth to the Gentiles, *without the intervention of the Apostles, or even of the Church at Jerusalem.* . . . Thus the development of the Church, assumes altogether the appearance of tending to set itself loose, and to separate, not merely from the Old Testament ordinance of the people of Israel, but even from the New Testament ordinance of the apostolate. The apostles understood how to reconcile this strange turn of things with their Lord's reign in heaven, and submitted to it willingly and joyfully. . . .

"Though the Christians of Antioch, considering the origin of their community, did not consider themselves as dependent in any way on the Apostles or on the Church of the first-fruits, but, on the contrary, knew that they were partakers of the same grace of God, and possessed the same immediate relation to the Lord as they did, still, on account of this very communion of grace, they felt a desire to become really conscious of this fellowship, and to acknowledge the position and dignity of the Apostles and of the Church at Jerusalem which had been assigned to them by the grace of their common Lord.

"As the first Gentile Church, looking on itself as at once the mother and natural representative of all Gentile Christian Churches, it sent a mission to Jerusalem, in order to learn how, in this opposite pole of the Christian world, they bore themselves with regard to the sect of the Pharisees, which had come from Jerusalem, and attempted to enforce Jewish ceremonies upon the Gentile Christians.

"The Church at Jerusalem, the mother of all the Churches in

Judea, Samaria, and Galilee, received the messengers from the Church at Antioch, which had introduced the discussion ; and every Gentile Christian saw in that Church (of Antioch) the maternal representative of all believers from the midst of the Gentiles.

"We see in this assembly, the two-foldness and free development of the Church, in its historical movement, and a representation of the whole Christian community, such as in the whole period of its development, it has never had, and never will have, again. . . . How are we to explain it, that the Apostles, with their superior knowledge and the authority committed to them, retire so far into the background, that *all present are to be thought of as taking part both in the deliberation and in the decision of the assembly ?*

"It becomes evident, that with the Apostles, it must have been a proximate object, to bring the several members of the community to self-conscious conviction on the whole of the disputable position which they had to discuss. They acted so as to allow the several members, perfect freedom of discussion, and to render it possible and easy for them by an independent act of their own judgment, to adopt the truth which was inherent in the matter.

"And from the Epistles it becomes still more evident that the Apostles did not come before the brethren, with their authority, in order to move them to adopt any particular line of conduct, but that *on all occasions they treated the different Churches, as capable of deciding for themselves.*"

"THE FIRST CHURCH IN EUROPE

consisted of the assembly of believers in the house of Lydia." This was the commencement of the Church of the Philippians, which St. Paul regarded as his " JOY AND CROWN," and to whose members he subsequently, so joyfully expressed his paternal affection in gratitude to God : " I thank my God upon every remembrance of you always in every prayer of mine, for you all, making request with joy for your fellowship in the gospel, from the first day until now."

"The first day" here referred to, was a golden day in the great Apostle's missionary career, as it is a red-letter day in the history of European Christendom.

"The man of Macedonia, who had appeared in vision to the Apostle, saying, "Come over and help us," fitly represented the collective presence of all the nations of the West. He, in effect, represented the Greek and Roman Empire, and confessed that *heathendom*, in the arts of Greece, and in the polity and Imperial power of Rome, *had arrived* at the end of *all its resources*. The Gentiles, with all the means of human nature and of earthly reality, had sought to gain salvation for themselves. But all had been in vain. Those who had gone farthest along the paths of natural development, were now pervaded by the feeling that all had indeed been vanity. This is the single pure result of all the history of heathendom.

"The man of Macedonia had called Paul and his companions, *to help the men of Europe*, in the desperate need in which they were then involved. . . .

"In this city of Philippi, therefore, in which Roman soldiers had been placed by Augustus (See Dio Cassius, as quoted by Kühnöl), and which had acquired not only the importance of an actual "colony," but also the '*jus Italicum*' besides, St. Paul halted, for the first time on his new career.

"Here, on the Sabbath day, on the banks of the Strymon, where prayer was wont to be made, the missionaries join the assembled women; for here, as elsewhere, the God-fearing among the Gentiles, who united with the Jews, in worshipping the true God, were chiefly females. And it is amongst these pious women the work of conversion was attended with such great results and blessing, as THE FIRST-FRUITS OF ST. PAUL'S LABOURS ON THE CONTINENT OF EUROPE.

"By the conversion of the house of Lydia, followed by that of the Philippian jailer and his family, a firm foundation was laid, on which the first Church in Europe might be built; and thereby the truth of the vision at Troas received its confirmation."

" From this centre and base of operations, the Apostle proceeded on his great missionary tour, for successful labour for the Evangelization of European Greece; and by these labours Christianity triumphed, when "the whole organization of the Roman Empire, from the omnipotent decrees of the Imperial city, down to the torturing stocks in the lowest cell of the remotest prison, was arrayed against the Gospel of Christ."

" If we ask why it is that Philippi not only made a glorious beginning, but also persevered, so that so late as the Apostle's imprisonment at Rome it was still his "joy and crown of rejoicing," we are referred once more to the two stable pillars of the Philippian Church, in the two households sanctified by faith. . . .

" By the Christian consecration of whole families, as the first-fruits of the Gentiles, which occurred at Philippi, the Gospel strikes its roots into the soil of nature, and secures to itself, on this soil, a development no less deeply moving than lasting."*

Note.—This first Christian Church in Europe, presented in the Inspired Record as a model Church, like that in Thessalonica (1 Thess. i. 7), was a Congregational fellowship, complete in its local organization, conducted by its own officers, "the bishops and deacons" (Phil. i. 1 ; ii. 1216.)

The able writer above quoted, remarking on the title of " Christians " as having originated amongst Gentile converts, but more particularly upon the regular observance of " the first day of the week" as " the Lord's Day," has the following :—

"Neander remarks very justly, that we must regard this festival as originating with the Gentile Christians, as Jewish

* *Baumgarten's* " Apostolic History," vol. ii. pp. 3, 12, 17, 117, 35, 141, 147.

Christians would naturally adhere to the Jewish Sabbath; and this observance of Sunday is a very characteristic feature of the Gentile Churches. . . .

"By conscientiously freeing themselves from the law of the Sabbath, they showed their living faith in Jesus, who had declared himself the 'Lord of the Sabbath.'

"On the other hand, however, it was shown that communities are not exempted from the observance of times, on account of the deliverance effected for them by Christ; and accordingly, even for the new life, an ordinance of times was necessary.

"In this transference of the festival from the seventh to the first day of the week, there is, even as Athanasius describes it, the element of the independence and freedom of the Gentile Churches, on the one hand, and on the other, the proof of their willingness to regulate their ordinances in deference to the laws and manners of their brethren, of the ancient people of God.

"We see in this, the far-reaching commencement of a normal system, in the Church of the Gentiles, which confined itself within those limits which had been laid down by the assembly at Jerusalem, for all times of the Gentile Church." *

Again, on the primitive custom of "breaking of bread together," he remarks: "By this solemn breaking of bread the Church represents itself as a family and household, meeting together at the same table; and this custom was founded, consequently, on the lively consciousness and enduring impression of the new life, in which all believers are created by one and the same spirit of God, and thereby formed into one family and brotherhood. . . .

"This sitting down at the same table, is, in the language of Scripture, the representation and realization of the highest and most perfect degree of fellowship among men. Here, for the first time, do Barbarians and Greeks, Asiatics and Europeans, Jews and Heathens, sit down at the same table, and are united in the spirit of communion and harmony. . . .

* ' Apostolic History," vol. ii. pp. 328, 329.

" For this community of the Church requires neither a people nor a country, neither the power nor the ordinances of a kingdom, but purely that which is everywhere furnished, by the personal existence of man upon the earth. . . .

"Out of the simple elements which are at hand wherever human beings exist, the house of God in the spirit may be built up. As in the house, the individual is ever recognized, and never can sink to the point of ultimate insignificance, so in the ecclesiastical form of communion, the individual soul remains in Christ, the ever-present ground and foundation of the life of the whole ; and on the other hand, even ' two or three ' represent the whole ; even as the whole, when it shall fill the whole world, shall have simply the form of the family and the household.

"For this reason, it is not a matter of accident, that *the smallest assembly bears the same holy name that belongs to the Universal Church.*" (Pp. 330–349.)

THE APOSTOLIC PLAN IN OPERATION.

" The idea set forth by Christ, of the union of His people with Himself and with one another, in one joint body, was kept alive by the Apostles. . . .

" The first arrangement in the newly-planted Churches, even the appointment of elders in them, was made by the Apostles themselves. Afterwards the officers belonging to societies of Christians were nominated by elders, with the consent of the Churches. . . .

"In many cities, the Churches were divided into several smaller communities, meeting in different places. In their assemblies there was an interchange of reading out of the Old Testament, explanation of what was read, free discourse, singing and prayer. The letters of Paul were also read and sent from one church to another. The Covenant Supper of Jesus was solemnized in an actual evening meal.

" The kiss of charity was customary, as the token of brotherly love in the assemblies.

"*Other regulations of the Churches were left free to each Society*, innocent national customs being observed, and therefore *they differed in separate communities.* . . .

"Still less was a distinct priestly order known at this time, for the whole society of Christians formed 'a royal priesthood,' God's peculiar people." * (1 Pet. v. 3.)

"It appears highly probable—I might say morally certain—that wherever a Jewish synagogue existed, that was brought—the whole, or the chief part of it—to embrace the Gospel, the Apostles did not there so much *form* a Christian Church, (or *congregation*, ecclesia) as *make an existing congregation Christian*, by introducing the Christian sacraments and worship, and establishing whatever regulations were necessary, leaving the existing machinery (if I may so speak) of government, unchanged.

"The attempt to effect this conversion of a Jewish Synagogue into a Christian Church, seems always to have been made in the first instance, in every place where there was an opening for it. . . . And when they founded a Church where there was no Jewish Synagogue that received the Gospel, it is likely they would still conform, in a great measure, to the same model."

"Although the many Churches which the Apostles founded were branches of one *spiritual* brotherhood, of which the Lord Jesus Christ is the heavenly head—though there was 'one Lord, one faith, one baptism,' for all of them—yet they were each a distinct, *independent* community on earth, united by the common principles on which they were founded, and by their mutual agreement, affection, and respect; but not having any one recognised Head on earth, or acknowledging any sovereignty of one of these societies over others.

"The plan pursued by the Apostles, seems to have been, to establish a great number of small distinct and independent communities, each governed by its own single bishop. . . .

* Geiseler's "Ecclesiastical History," vol. i. pp. 90–92.

" Generally speaking, the Apostles appear to have clearly established a distinct Church in each considerable city; so that there were several even in a single province; as, for instance, in Macedonia, those of Philippi, Thessalonica, Berœa, Amphipolis, &c.; and the like in the province of Achaia, and elsewhere.

" Again, it seems plainly to have been at least the general, if not the universal, practice of the Apostles to appoint, over each separate Church, a single individual as a chief governor, under the title of 'Angel' (*i.e.* Messenger, or Legate from the Apostles), or Bishop, *i.e.* 'Superintendent or Overseer.' A Church and a Diocese seem to have been for a considerable time coextensive and identical. And each Church or Diocese, (and consequently each Superintendent), though connected with the rest, by ties of Faith and Hope and Charity, seems to have been (as has been already observed) *perfectly independent as regards any power of control.*

" EACH CHURCH, therefore, was left, through the wise fore-sight of Him who alone ' knew what was in man,' to provide for it own wants as they should arise; to steer its own course, *by the chart and compass which His holy Word supplies;* regulating for itself, the sails and rudder, according to the winds and currents it may meet with."—*Archbishop Whateley,* " Essays on the Kingdom of Christ," pp. 40, 47, 102, 103, 129, 247.

" The Holy Ghost, through His agents, the Apostles, has not left any detailed account of the formation of any Christian society; but *He has very distinctly marked the great principles on which all were to be founded,* whatever distinctions may exist amongst them. In short, the foundation of the Church, by the Apostles, was not analagous to the work of Romulus or Solon; it was not, properly, the foundation of Christian socie-ties that occupied them, but the establishment of THE PRIN-CIPLES, *on which Christians, in all ages, might form societies for themselves.*" — " Encyclopedia Metropolitana," " Age of Apostolic Fathers," p. 774.

CONCLUSION.

"I set myself seriously to inquire into the controversies then warmly agitated in these nations. Of the Congregational way I was not acquainted with any one person, minister or other; nor had I, to my knowledge, seen any more than *one* in my life. My acquaintance lay wholly with ministers and people of the Presbyterian way. But sundry books being published on either side, I perused them and compared them with the Scripture and one another, according as I received ability from God. After a general view of them, as was my manner in other controversies, I fixed on one to take under peculiar consideration and examination, which seemed most methodically and strongly to maintain that which was contrary, as I thought, to my present persuasion. This was Mr. Cotton's book 'Of the Keys.' The examination and confutation hereof, merely for my own particular satisfaction, with what diligence and sincerity I was able, I engaged in. What progress I made in that undertaking, I can manifest unto any, by the discourses on that subject, and animadversions on that book, yet abiding by me. *In the pursuit and management of this work, quite beside and contrary to my expectation, at a time and season wherein I could expect nothing on that account but ruin in this world, without the knowledge or advice of, or conference with any one person of that judgment, I was prevailed on to receive that and those principles which I had thought to have set myself in opposition unto.* AND, INDEED, THIS WAY OF IMPARTIAL EXAMINING ALL THINGS BY THE WORD, COMPARING CAUSES WITH CAUSES, AND THINGS WITH THINGS, LAYING ASIDE ALL PREJUDICATE RESPECTS UNTO PERSONS, OR PRESENT TRADITIONS, IS A COURSE THAT I WOULD ADMONISH ALL TO BEWARE OF, WHO WOULD AVOID THE DANGER OF BECOMING INDEPENDENTS."—*Rev. John Owen, D.D.,* Author of "Exposition of Hebrews," Works, vol. xix. p. 274.

PUBLIC WORSHIP.

———•———

" God is a Spirit: and they that worship Him, must worship Him in spirit and in truth."

" Let us draw near, with a true heart, in full assurance of faith."

———

PERSONS attending a place of Christian Worship, ought to be present *punctually*, at the COMMENCEMENT of each service, or A LITTLE EARLIER ; that they may wait upon God without distraction, and that they may avoid disturbing others.

They should *unite* in the Worship of God, by accompanying, in THOUGHT and DESIRE, those who audibly lead the devotions; and not merely LISTEN while others sing and pray.

They should devoutly and intelligently EXPRESS their participation in worship, by *audibly* uttering the " Amen " and other responses to prayer, and by UNITING IN SINGING the praises of God, with harmony and decorum.

They should generally *kneel* or STAND at prayer, and stand up for singing (except in cases of infirmity or inconvenience), and sit, only when they are to read or listen.

They should carefully avoid *drowsiness* and WANDERING OF MIND, and all levity and restlessness of demeanour, which would hinder devotion, in themselves or in others.

5

They should listen, *reverently*, to THE WORD OF GOD, and candidly consider what is spoken by their fellow-men, in God's name, for their benefit.

They should *meditate* upon what they hear, and " search the Scriptures " for themselves, with FERVENT PRAYER, that they may be " taught of God," and made " wise unto salvation, through faith which is in Christ Jesus."

They should receive the truth *practically*, in a loving and obedient spirit ; and honestly act upon convictions of duty, avoiding every evil way, and cordially uniting with those who love Christ, in efforts to obey His commands and glorify His name.

They should endeavour to induce *others* to attend the house of God; and cheerfully contribute of their time, their influence, and their money, to maintain the interests of religion, where they worship, and to promote the knowledge and blessings of the Gospel in the world.

————

"Let us have grace, whereby we may serve God acceptably, with reverence and godly fear."

"Oh come, let us worship and bow down; let us kneel before the Lord our Maker.

"Let us come before His presence with thanksgiving, and make a joyful noise unto Him with psalms."

"To-day if ye will hear His voice, harden not your hearts."

ABOUT THE "ANCIENT CATHOLIC FAITH,"

AND HOW THE UNIVERSAL CHURCH DID WITHOUT THE PAPACY.

———◆◆———

THE close of the Apostles' ministry marked an important era in the history of the Christian Church. A glance at the facts will disclose a most interesting and critical state of affairs.

Already, many sad cases of defection from truth and purity, had occurred, amongst the Churches which had been planted by the Apostles. In the face of apostolic authority and miraculous gifts, some had "already turned aside after Satan." Many forms of error, false doctrine, and corruption had appeared, and even "the mystery of iniquity" was already working.

The Apostles had warned and admonished the Churches, "even with tears," beseeching them to "stand fast in the faith," and resist these beginnings of apostacy; but still the evil continued, and with the most solemn and affecting admonitions, these holy men uttered startling predictions of "perilous times," and lamentable declension, perversion, and confusion, as coming upon the infant Church, from which they were about to be removed by death.

Nothing can be more patent and impressive than this part of apostolic testimony. It challenges attention, and suggests inquiry, from the most cursory observer of the facts.

The sure word of prophecy, which promises the ultimate triumph of truth, and predicts the glory of the Redeemer's kingdom, is not more explicit than are the reiterations of apostolic warning, about the spread and fatal prevalence of corruption and apostacy—*already begun!*

Here a most important inquiry presses itself, upon every candid and thoughtful mind. How did the Apostles instruct the Churches to provide against the " perilous times," of which they gave such solemn warning ?   By what methods did they prepare the Christian converts and their teachers, to defend themselves and society, against the assaults of error and corruption, thus foreseen and deplored ?   They predict the deluge, —how do they describe the ark ?

If ever an infallible human authority was necessary, as supreme ruler of the Universal Church, it was—*just then!* When the inspired Apostles were passing away, and the canon of Scripture was not yet completed, and there was no Christian literature, and creeds and rubrics had not yet been compiled, and the new faith was coming into contact with various forms of civilization, barbarism, and national life, and new converts from Heathenism and Judaism were but defectively educated, and errors and false teachers were abounding—*then*, surely, *then, if ever*—we should find distinct, emphatic, authoritative mention of—the Pope !

But where is " his Holiness " introduced by the inspired Apostles ?   In all their writings where and how is this important personage—the official ruler and supreme head of the Church—described ?

We search for him in vain through all the apostolic writings, (unless we are content to find him in a wrong place !)   The New Testament Churches know nothing of him.   He is not in the book of the Acts of the Apostles, or in the Epistle to the Romans, or anywhere else in the Divine record.

The Apostles do not reveal him, predict him, *or leave room for him,* in their instructions to the Churches.   Paul and Jude, Peter, James, and John, all instructed and admonished Christians, regarding " deceivers," " false apostles," " evil workers " " drawing away disciples after them," " overthrowing the faith of some," and " making shipwreck of the faith." The last warning voice heard from them is : " Even now there are many Antichrists."   But they gave no hint of the presence, advent, authority, or functions of Christ's vicegerent, the infallible director of the Universal Church, whose " ex cathedrâ " utterances, in Bull, or Syllabus, or Decree, are to preserve the faithful in truth and unity.   On the contrary, they spoke and wrote, *as no honest and well-informed men could have spoken and written, if they had known the Papacy to be an essential part of Christianity.*

This demands the most serious consideration of all who

profess and call themselves Christians. How is it to be explained?

Did Peter know that he was the first Pope? Could he have been the head of the clerical dynasty, divinely ordained to rule the Church in all ages, and not know it? If he did not know it, how did others come to know it? If he did know it, his pontifical consecration did not prevent his becoming an arch-traitor to the Divine purpose; for he has, in that case, written his two Epistles, so as to conceal Christianity, and deceive men, regarding the wisdom and beneficence of God.

Did the other Apostles know of the universal episcopate, begun in Peter, and to be continued in unbroken succession, in kingly priests, holding dominion in Rome?

Then they conspired with Peter, to cheat the world out of the bequest of omnipotent mercy!

Peter distinctly speaks of "lying teachers bringing in sects of perdition;" and sadly predicts that "many shall follow their riotousness, through whom the way of truth shall be evil spoken of" (2nd Epistle ii. 2, &c., Douay Testament); and as a faithful shepherd he lovingly tries to save the flock. But how? Hear him: "I think it meet, as long as I am in this tabernacle, to stir you up, by putting you in remembrance;" and "I will do my endeavour, that *after my decease* also, you may often have whereby you may keep a memory of these things."

Here is St. Peter's purpose; but where is the Pope? Was it hypocritical pretence, forgetfulness, cowardice, treachery, that kept the venerable Apostle from enjoining obedience and submission to "the supreme pontiff," his successor?

Can any one imagine that Peter knew the Papacy to be a Divine ordinance, and yet *made no allusion to it, when doing his endeavour, to secure the well-being of the Church, after his decease!* True, he speaks of "the Prince of pastors"—but he alludes to the glorified Redeemer, the head of the Church, in heaven. He knew of no other infallible head of the Church. His teaching leaves no place for another. The Christianity of St. Peter is complete *without* THE POPE.

And so of all his fellow-workers, the Apostles of our Lord and Saviour. When delivering their most solemn instructions, by Divine inspiration, *on the very subjects that required explicit mention of "the Vicar of Christ"* (if they had known of such a person), no intimation, recognition, or prediction of any such officer in Christ's kingdom, escapes from them. They distinctly inform us *how* the Lord, when He ascended up on high, provided " for the perfecting of the saints, for the work of the ministry, for the edifying of the body of Christ." They declare that " He gave some apostles, some prophets, and other some evangelists, and other some pastors and doctors, or teachers " (Ephes. iv. 8-14, Douay Testament), but not a a word about the Pope !

These holy men, moved by the Holy Ghost, to instruct and admonish the Churches, in the things of the kingdom of God, beseech and warn them against being " carried away by every wind of doctrine, by the wickedness of men, by the cunning craftiness by which they lie in wait to deceive." But at this very point where the Papacy ought to come in, it is conspicuously left out.

The Apostles knew nothing of it. It is not revealed, promised, or provided for, in the dispensation of the Gospel, revealed to all nations " for the obedience of faith."

How, then, did the Universal Church, by apostolic teaching, *do without the Papacy?* Simply by taking heed to apostolic doctrine. On this point Catholic apostolic injunction is clear and emphatic.

As with one voice these holy men admonish Christians, " That ye be mindful of the words which were spoken before by the holy prophets, and of the commandments of us, the apostles of the Lord and Saviour " (Peter).

" As ye have received Jesus Christ the Lord, so walk in Him ; rooted and built up in Him, and confirmed in the faith, as you have been taught." " Beware lest any man *cheat* you." " Your faith should not stand in the wisdom of men, but in the power of God." " Though we or an angel from heaven preach a gospel to you, besides that which we have preached to you, let him be anathema " (Paul). " If any of you want wisdom, let him ask of God, who giveth to all men abundantly." " Of His own will hath He begotten us, *by the word of truth.*" " Be ye doers of the word " (James). " Let that which you have heard *from the beginning,* abide in you." " I have not written to you as to those that know not the truth ; but as to them that know it, and that no lie is of the truth " (John). " Building yourselves up in your most holy faith, praying in the Holy Ghost, keep yourselves in the love of God" (Jude). "Trust perfectly in the grace which is offered you in the revelation of Jesus Christ." "Being born again, not of corruptible seed, but incorruptible, *by the word God*." "The word of the Lord endureth for ever, and this is the word which by the Gospel hath been preached unto you." "If any man speak, let him speak as the words of God" (Peter, Douay Testament).

Thus, the Apostles taught the Universal Church, in the most critical time of its history, to do without the Papacy. In all their instructions, admonitions, encouragements, given to the disciples of Christ, about resisting error and maintaining the truth, we find not a hint of any centre of unity on earth, or of any mortal invested with the function of presiding over the faithful, and claiming submission to his decisions, as articles of faith. Instead of this, we find just such directions as Christians everywhere now may adopt and enjoy, without the Pope's permission, and even despite his hostility and his curse.

Nay, further, it is important to observe, that we of the present age, are far better prepared to resist error, more qualified to defend the truth, and maintain purity in the Churches, than the early Christians were. We can do without the Pope much better than they could; yet it is unquestionable that they who most needed him, had to do without him. He was not invented until it was too late.

The Papacy is a *growth* of the post-apostolic ages, and its parentage and history are full of interest and instruction. Although it originated in efforts to bridle and reform some of the early corruptions of "Catholic antiquity," and has often done good service, in laying the strong hand of repression upon rampant abominations, yet its authority is *not* of God. It is at best, a human device, in imitation of worldly power. It is a usurpation in Christ's kingdom. It is Cæsarism in the Church. It has had its day, as a sacerdotal child's play at empire. But it has survived its era, and "that which decayeth and waxeth old is ready to vanish away."

The world knows that what has been facetiously called "the Chair of St. Peter" is but a ricketty, rotten relic of the long empty throne of the Emperors of the West; and mankind now, in all civilized nations, regard with amazement or amusement, the assumptions of an "Infallible Papacy," which they know to be a fading phantom—the ephemeral " last edition" or newest style, "just out," of the PONTIFEX MAXIMUS of old Pagan Rome!

Not so the true and ancient Catholic faith—the Divine old faith, ever new, as " the Word of our God," which " shall stand for ever." It abideth throughout the ages ; and to-day, as in the olden time, its glory shines upon the nations, and all men may read, as in the light of heaven—that

" GOD SO LOVED THE WORLD THAT HE GAVE HIS ONLY-BEGOTTEN SON, THAT WHOSOEVER BELIEVETH IN HIM SHOULD NOT PERISH, BUT HAVE EVERLASTING LIFE."

This is the " glorious Gospel "—the ancient Catholic faith, by which God will bless and save the nations.

Our inquiry has been, exclusively of apostolic teaching and the apostolic age. To any who may desire to look farther, a conclusive test is at hand, and it can be applied without tedious critical research in ecclesiastical history. The Papacy has preserved the proof of its own usurpation and apostacy. All Christendom is familiar with " the three Creeds." These formularies, designated severally (though inaccurately), as " The Apostles' Creed," " The Nicene Creed," and " The Athanasian Creed," set forth formally and by authority, summaries of " orthodox " belief, accepted and enforced, by the majority of professed Christians, including the Church of Rome, from the fourth to the sixteenth century, and since.

Here is the voice of so-called " Catholic antiquity " dogmatically proclaiming the faith, through the ages. *It is silent about the Papacy !* No sound is given, of an infallible human authority, ruling the Universal Church. It has no recognition of the Pope. Nay, more, even when the Papacy, which accepted these three Creeds, forged a fourth, to cover its own corruptions, it did not venture to claim a place for itself, *within the domain of faith.* In its palmiest days of despotic rule, it was only an administrative function—a form of government. " The Church," it was said, " possesses infallibility," though Popes may err.

The usurpation that set itself up outside the Church, on the unconsecrated ground of worldly dominion, now demands that its title to INFALLIBILITY and SUPREMACY, shall be accepted as an article of the Christian faith. Catholic antiquity denies the claim !